Nifty Thrifty Crafts for Kids

Nifty Thrifty
ANIMAL
Crafts

Faith K. Gabriel

Enslow Elementary

an imprint of

 Enslow Publishers, Inc.

40 Industrial Road
Box 398
Berkeley Heights, NJ 07922
USA

http://www.enslow.com

To my family with love—FKG

Enslow Elementary, an imprint of Enslow Publishers, Inc.

Enslow Elementary® is a registered trademark of Enslow Publishers, Inc.

Library of Congress Cataloging-in-Publication Data

Gabriel, Faith K.
   Nifty thrifty animal crafts / Faith K. Gabriel. — 1st ed.
     p. cm. — (Nifty thrifty crafts for kids)
   Includes bibliographical references and index.
   ISBN-13: 978-0-7660-2779-4
   ISBN-10: 0-7660-2779-1
   1. Handicraft—Juvenile literature. 2. Animals in art—Juvenile literature. I. Title. II. Series.
TT160.G22 2007
745.5—dc22

2006005907

Printed in the United States of America

10 9 8 7 6 5 4 3 2

To Our Readers: We have done our best to make sure all Internet Addresses in this book were active and appropriate when we went to press. However, the author and the publisher have no control over and assume no liability for the material available on those Internet sites or on other Web sites they may link to. Any comments or suggestions can be sent by e-mail to comments@enslow.com or to the address on the back cover.

Safety Note: Be sure to ask for help from an adult, if needed, to complete these crafts!

Contents

Animals have lived on Earth for millions of years, and new ones are still being discovered. It would be difficult to study all of them without some way of grouping, or classifying, them. To make it easier, scientists group animals together that have something in common.

For example, scientists can classify animals by their bones. If an animal has a spine, or backbone, it is a member of the vertebrate group. Fish, dogs, and cats are vertebrates. Animals without backbones, such as butterflies, worms, and spiders, are invertebrates. Most of the animals on Earth belong to the invertebrate group.

Another way of classifying animals is if they are warm-blooded or cold-blooded. A warm-blooded animal is one whose inside body temperature stays the same no matter how hot or cold it is outside. Monkeys and birds are warm-blooded animals.

Cold-blooded animals are animals that cannot control their body temperature. When it is cold outside, their inside body temperature gets cold. When it is hot outside, their inside body temperature gets hot. Snakes and frogs are cold-blooded animals.

A third way to classify animals is by what they eat. Are they herbivores or carnivores or omnivores? Herbivores are plant eaters. Deer and giraffes are herbivores. Carnivores are meat eaters. Sharks and lions are carnivores. Omnivores eat both plants and meat. Pigs and raccoons are omnivores.

The crafts in this book are all about different animals. Have fun learning some new things about the world of animals as you make these crafts.

Pet Photo Frame

Are You Ready?

There are almost 140 million dogs and cats kept as pets in the United States. Many pet owners love their animals so much that they have photographs of them around the house. Make a frame for a pet's photograph. You can even make a frame to give as a gift.

Get Set

- ✔ thin cardboard
- ✔ ruler
- ✔ pencil
- ✔ scissors
- ✔ aluminum foil
- ✔ colored paper
- ✔ white glue
- ✔ pet photograph (Ask permission first!)

Let's Go!

1. Cut a 6-inch by 8-inch piece of cardboard. Fold it in half (see A).

2. Gently squeeze the foil into a loose ball. Open it up and smooth the foil.

3. Fold the foil over the top and bottom of the frame (see B).

4. Then fold the foil over the sides of the frame. Tuck under the corners for a neat finish (see C).

5. Cut the colored paper a little larger than the photograph.

6. Glue the photograph to the center of the paper. Let dry (see D).

7. Glue the photograph on the paper in the center of the frame (see E). Let dry. Display your pet's photograph in your room or where all can see it.

Safety Note: Be sure to ask for help from an adult, if needed, to complete these crafts!

A

B

C

D

E

Floppy Fish Bookmark

Are You Ready?

Some fish are named for other animals. There are batfish, butterfly fish, catfish, dogfish, goatfish, goosefish, porcupine fish, scorpion fish, squirrelfish, toadfish, and wolffish!

Get Set

- ✔ **thin cardboard**
- ✔ **pencil**
- ✔ **scissors**
- ✔ **markers**
- ✔ **white glue**

Safety Note: Be sure to ask for help from an adult, if needed, to complete these crafts!

Let's Go!

1. On thin cardboard, draw a fish. (See page 28 for the pattern.) Cut the fish out.

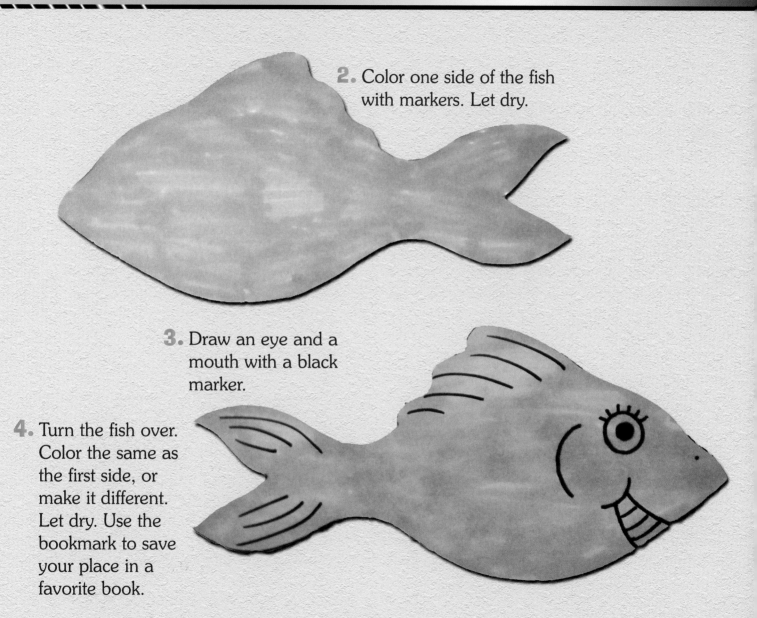

2. Color one side of the fish with markers. Let dry.

3. Draw an eye and a mouth with a black marker.

4. Turn the fish over. Color the same as the first side, or make it different. Let dry. Use the bookmark to save your place in a favorite book.

Turtle Crayon Holder

Are You Ready?

When a mother turtle lays eggs, she buries them in a nest and leaves them. The eggs have to hatch by themselves. Most of the eggs will hatch into more female turtles if the temperature around the nest is warm. If it is cooler, the eggs will hatch into more male turtles.

Get Set

✔ **thin cardboard**

✔ **pencil**

✔ **scissors**

✔ **markers**

✔ **colored paper**

✔ **4-ounce empty can (snack size)**

✔ **white glue**

✔ **crayons**

Safety Note: Be sure to ask for help from an adult, if needed, to complete these crafts!

Let's Go!

1. On thin cardboard, draw a turtle. (See page 27 for the pattern.) Cut it out.

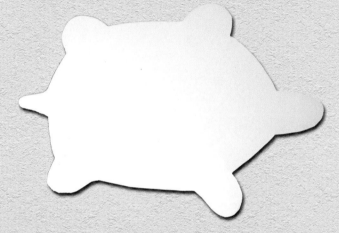

2. Color the turtle's back with markers.

3. Cut a strip of colored paper to fit around the can. Decorate the paper strip with markers.

4. Glue the paper strip around the can. Let dry.

5. Put glue on the bottom of the can. Glue the can in the center of the turtle's back. Let dry overnight.

6. Put your crayons in the holder.

11

Favorite Animal Necklace

Cats are the most popular pets in the United States. Other favorite animals are dogs, birds, rabbits, gerbils, hamsters, fish, and reptiles, such as snakes and turtles.

Get Set

- ✔ plastic lid from a food container
- ✔ hole punch
- ✔ permanent markers
- ✔ colored paper scrap
- ✔ scissors
- ✔ animal photograph (Ask permission first!)
- ✔ white glue
- ✔ yarn

Let's Go!

1. Ask an adult to help you punch a hole at the top of the lid or on the rim. Decorate the front of the rim with permanent markers (see A).

2. Cut a piece of colored paper to fit in the center of the lid (see B). Glue the paper on the lid (see C). Let dry.

3. Trim the photograph so that it is a little smaller than the colored paper. Glue the photograph on the colored paper. Make sure the hole in the lid is at the top of the photograph. Let dry.

4. Cut a piece of yarn about 26 inches long to fit over your head when it is tied. Put one end through the hole in the lid. Then tie the ends together (see D). Wear the necklace or give it as a gift.

Safety Note: Be sure to ask for help from an adult, if needed, to complete these crafts!

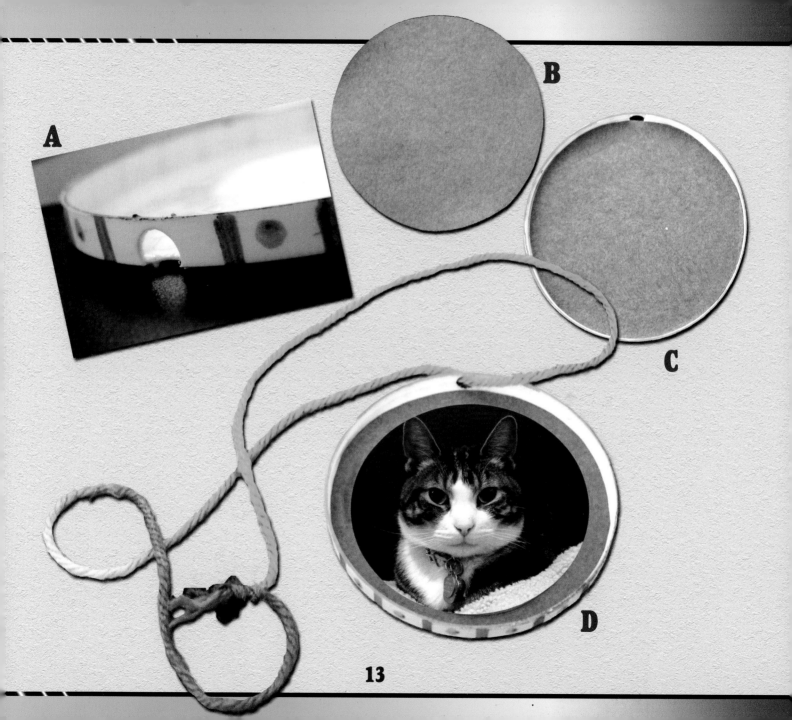

A

B

C

D

13

Flying Bird Ornament

There are about ten thousand kinds of birds in the world. The largest bird is the ostrich. It can grow to nine feet tall and weigh over three hundred pounds. The smallest bird is the bee hummingbird. It weighs about half an ounce and is almost two inches long. It is about the same size as the eye of an ostrich.

Get Set

- ✔ construction paper
- ✔ pencil
- ✔ ruler
- ✔ markers
- ✔ scissors
- ✔ stapler
- ✔ clear tape
- ✔ hole punch
- ✔ yarn
- ✔ colored paper scrap
- ✔ two small paper clips

Let's Go!

1. Cut a piece of construction paper 6 inches by 7 inches. Draw a line 1 inch from the edge of both long sides of the paper for the borders. Decorate the borders with markers (see A).

2. Fold the paper in half the long way with the borders on the outside. Starting at the fold, cut thirteen strips as wide as your finger up to the border line (see B). At the border line, cut off every other strip to make the cage (see C).

3. Open up the cage and bend it around. Staple or tape the ends together.

4. Punch a hole in one border at the top. Punch a second hole opposite the first hole. Put a piece of yarn through the holes and knot the ends together.

5. On colored paper, draw a bird. (See page 27 for the pattern.)

6. Open up a paper clip. Tape the clip to the bird (see D). Slide a second paper clip onto the first one. Hook the second clip on the yarn inside the cage. Hang the bird ornament in your room or on the refrigerator (see E).

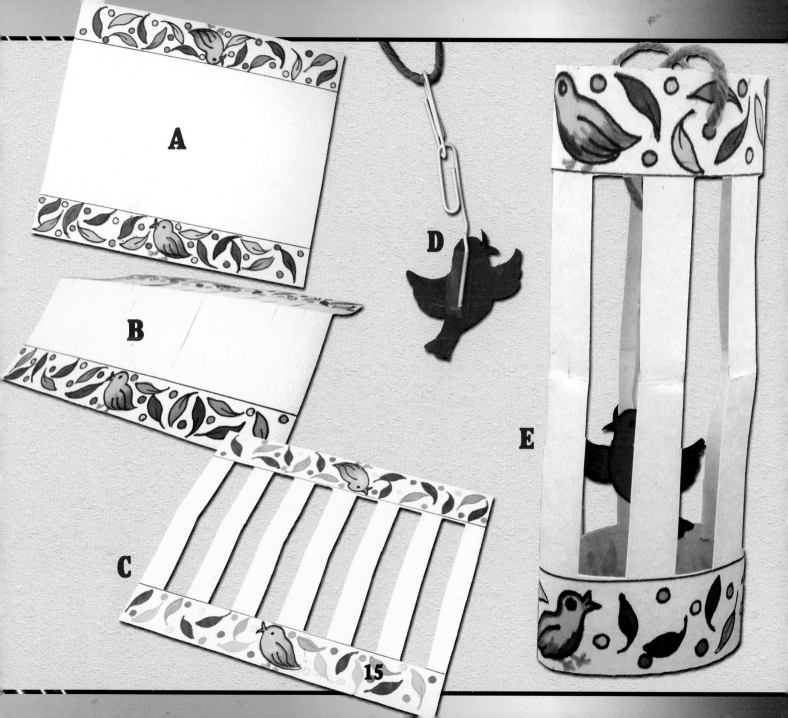

A

B

C

D

E

15

Monkey Pencil Box

Are You Ready?

Monkeys use sounds, make faces, and use body language to communicate. They stare, slap their hands on the ground, or show their teeth when they are angry. Their screeches, yells, cries, and chatter are all messages about danger, finding food, and their home territory.

Get Set

- ✔ white paper
- ✔ pencil
- ✔ construction paper
- ✔ white glue
- ✔ scissors
- ✔ markers
- ✔ empty cereal box
- ✔ ruler

Let's Go!

1. On white paper, draw the monkeys. (See page 26 for the pattern.) Glue the pattern on a sheet of construction paper. Let dry. Cut out the pattern (see A).

2. Color the monkeys with markers. Leave the ears and face white (see B).

3. Cut a piece from the bottom of a cereal box about 2 inches high. This will be the pencil box. Cut a strip of colored paper to go around the four sides of the pencil box. Glue the paper on the box and let dry.

4. Glue the monkeys to the inside back of the pencil box. Let dry. Make a "My Pencils" sign. Glue the sign to the front of the box. Let dry (see C). Put your pencils in the box.

Safety Note: Be sure to ask for help from an adult, if needed, to complete these crafts!

16

A

B

C

17

Do Not Disturb Shark Sign

Are You Ready?

A shark's teeth grow all during its life. When a tooth breaks or falls out, another tooth fills its place. Some sharks can have as many as three thousand teeth set in about five rows at one time. Their sharp teeth tear food into large pieces to eat whole without chewing.

Get Set

- ✔ **pencil**
- ✔ **thin and thick cardboard**
- ✔ **scissors**
- ✔ **black marker**
- ✔ **blue paper**
- ✔ **white glue**
- ✔ **hole punch**
- ✔ **yarn**
- ✔ **small plastic bottle cap**

Let's Go!

1. Draw a shark on thin cardboard. (See page 28 for the pattern.) Cut it out.

2. Use the black marker to outline all around the edges of the shark.

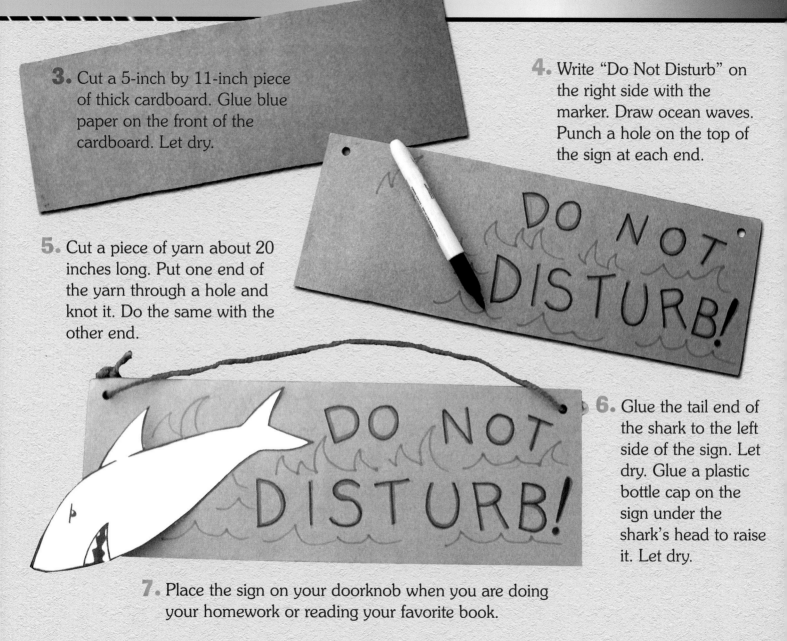

3. Cut a 5-inch by 11-inch piece of thick cardboard. Glue blue paper on the front of the cardboard. Let dry.

4. Write "Do Not Disturb" on the right side with the marker. Draw ocean waves. Punch a hole on the top of the sign at each end.

5. Cut a piece of yarn about 20 inches long. Put one end of the yarn through a hole and knot it. Do the same with the other end.

6. Glue the tail end of the shark to the left side of the sign. Let dry. Glue a plastic bottle cap on the sign under the shark's head to raise it. Let dry.

7. Place the sign on your doorknob when you are doing your homework or reading your favorite book.

Animal Treasure Box

Are You Ready?

People protect important things in special boxes called safes. You can protect your treasures in a special box, too.

Get Set

✔ **box with a lid**

✔ **construction paper**

✔ **scissors**

✔ **white glue**

✔ **pictures of animals from old magazines (Ask permission first!)**

✔ **shiny pennies to decorate the sides of the box (Ask permission first!)**

Let's Go!

1. Cut a piece of construction paper to cover the top of the box lid. Glue the paper on the lid. Let dry.

2. Cut out pictures of all different animals. Glue the pictures on the lid. Let dry.

3. Glue pennies on the sides of the lid and box. Work on one side at a time. Let each side dry overnight before starting on the next side.

4. Once everything is dry, place your treasures in the box for safekeeping.

Safety Note: Be sure to ask for help from an adult, if needed, to complete these crafts!

Silver Giraffe Sculpture

As the tallest land animals, giraffes can eat up to 140 pounds of food each day. Their 18-inch tongues wrap around branches to strip off leaves from trees and bushes. There is enough water in their food so they can go for a couple of weeks without drinking. When they do find water, they may drink as much as 12 gallons at one time.

Get Set

- ✔ picture of a giraffe
- ✔ aluminum foil
- ✔ small box, such as one for bar soap
- ✔ clear tape
- ✔ colored paper
- ✔ scissors
- ✔ white glue
- ✔ marker

Let's Go!

1. Look at a picture of a giraffe. Notice its shape and body parts.

2. Tear off a long piece of aluminum foil. Squeeze it into the shape of the giraffe's body (see A).

3. Add long pieces of foil for the other giraffe parts. Squeeze the pieces to attach them to the giraffe's body and to shape them (see B). Use your fingers to make small parts such as ears.

4. Tape the ends of a small box closed. Glue on colored paper to cover the box (see C). Let dry.

5. Make a small sign for the sculpture on a scrap of paper. Glue it on the front of the box. Let dry. Glue the sculpture on the top of the box (see D). Let dry overnight.

6. Put your giraffe on display. What other animals can you make with foil?

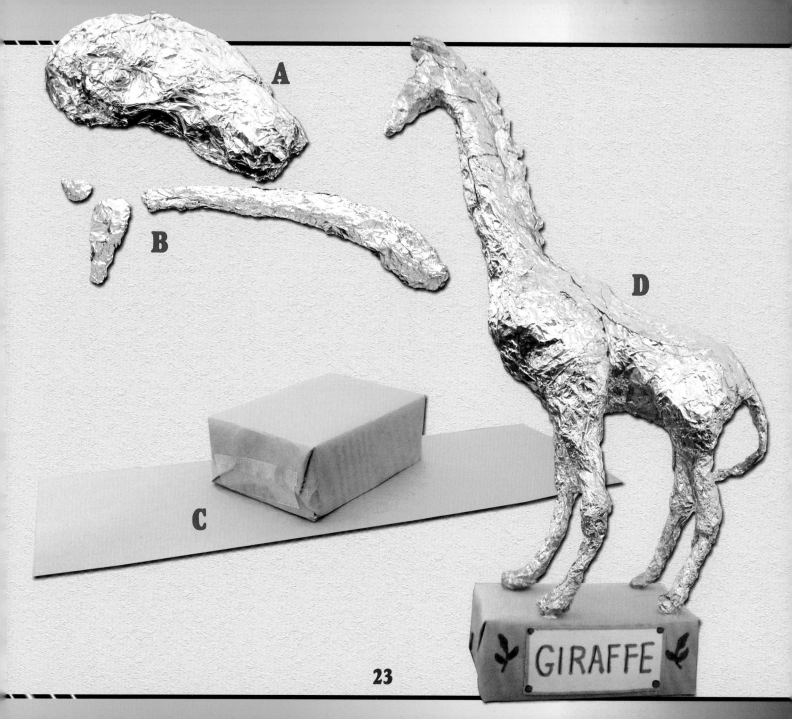

A

B

C

D

GIRAFFE

23

Butterfly Flutter Fan

Are You Ready?

Butterflies use their body parts in unexpected ways. To taste food, they stand on their six legs and feet. They cannot bite or chew, so they drink their food through a strawlike tube called a proboscis. They breathe through openings in their body. Their antennas are used for their sense of smell, and they hear sounds through their colorful wings.

Get Set

- ✔ **pencil**
- ✔ **thin cardboard**
- ✔ **scissors**
- ✔ **markers**
- ✔ **cotton swab**
- ✔ **white glue**

Let's Go!

1. On thin cardboard, draw a large butterfly. (See page 29 for the pattern.) Cut it out (see A).

2. Use markers to color designs on the butterfly's wings.

3. Decorate the back side of the butterfly the same as the front, or make it different.

4. Break a cotton swab in half. Color each half with a black marker (see B). Let dry.

5. Glue the two pieces on the top of the butterfly for antennas. Let dry (see C).

6. Place the flutter fan between your thumb and first finger. Gently wave it back and forth (see D).

A

B

C

D

25

Patterns

Use tracing paper to copy the patterns on these pages. Ask an adult to help you cut and trace the shapes onto construction paper.

Monkey Pencil Box
at 100%

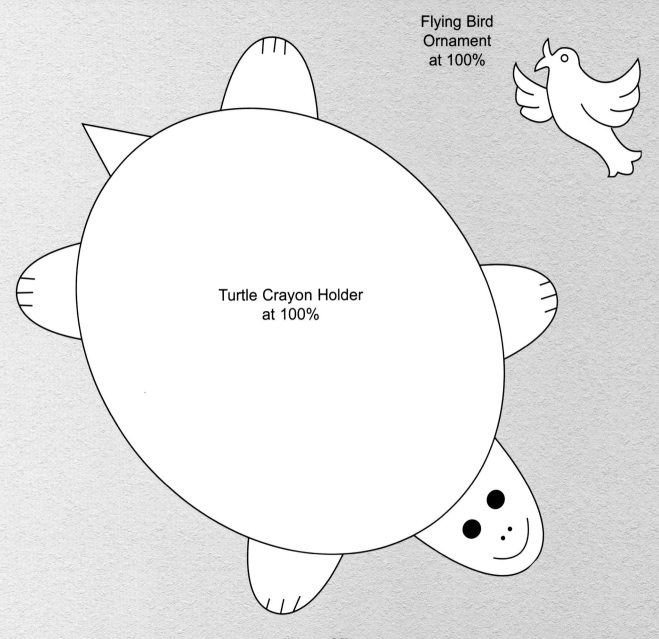

Flying Bird
Ornament
at 100%

Turtle Crayon Holder
at 100%

27

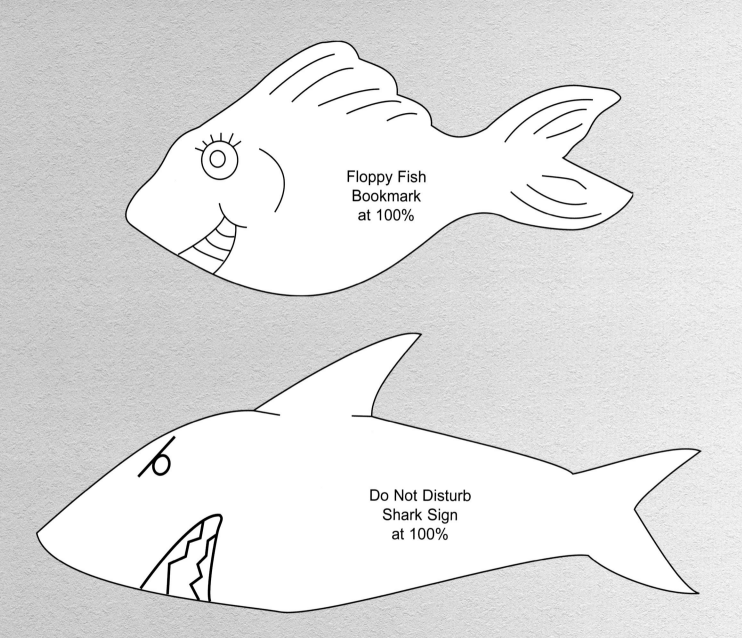

Floppy Fish
Bookmark
at 100%

Do Not Disturb
Shark Sign
at 100%

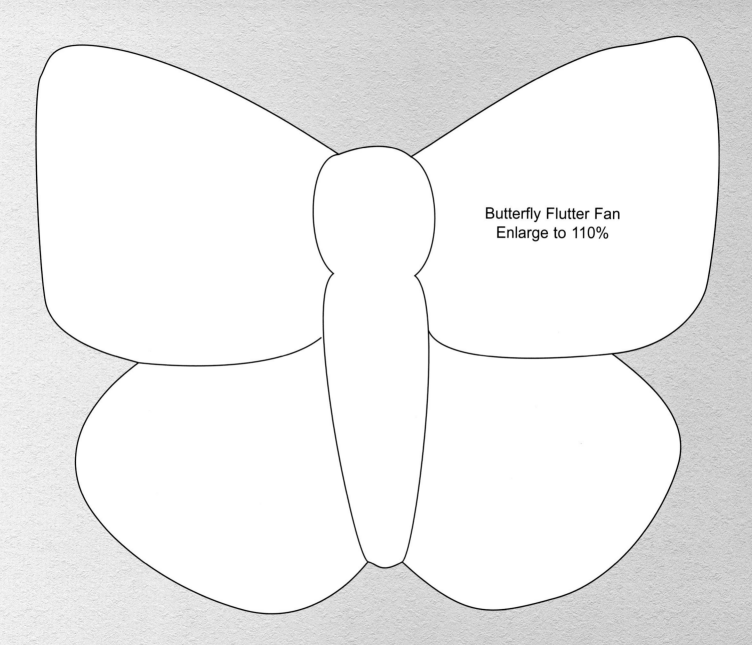

Butterfly Flutter Fan
Enlarge to 110%

29

Reading About

Books

Baillie, Marilyn. *Amazing Things Animals Do*. Toronto, Canada: Maple Tree Press, 2003.

Harvey, Bev. *Reptiles*. Philadelphia, Penn.: Chelsea Clubhouse Books, 2003.

Hickman, Pamela. *Animals in Motion: How Animals Swim, Jump, Slither and Glide*. Toronto, Canada: Kids Can Press, 2000.

Lundbald, Kristina, and Bobbie Kalman. *Animals Called Fish*. New York: Crabtree Pub. Co., 2005.

Press, Judy. *At the Zoo!: Explore the Animal World with Craft Fun*. Charlotte, Vt.: Williamson Pub., 2002.

Simon, Seymour. *Animals Nobody Loves*. New York: SeaStar Books, 2001.

Internet Addresses

ASPCA'S Animaland

<http://www.animaland.org>

This site has games and information on pet care, careers, and animals in general.

Defenders of Wildlife—Kids' Planet

<http://www.kidsplanet.org>

There are many interesting activities and facts relating to wildlife on this site.

Index